# First-Place Reading

# PHONICS PRACTICE READER

## GRADE 1

ISBN 0-15-334591-8

2 3 4 5 6 7 8 9 10   179   10 09 08 07 06 05 04 03 02

# CONTENTS

**It's Hot** . . . . . . . . . . . . . . . **5**
Phonic Element: /o/o

**Shortstop and the Bug** . . . **13**
Phonic Elements: /th/*th*; /sh/*sh*

**A Big Hit** . . . . . . . . . . . . **21**
Phonic Elements: *Blends with s, r, l*

# CONTENTS

**Pig's Good Morning** . . . . **29**
Phonic Element: /ôr/or

**What a Kick!** . . . . . . . . . **37**
Contractions: n't, 'll, 're

# It's Hot

by Megan Casey

Illustrations
by Pam Levy

Tom sat on top.

"It's hot," said Dot. "Come
sit on top," said Tom.

"It's hot. Too hot,"
said Don.

"It's not hot here,"
said Dot. "Come sit
on top," said Tom.

"I am hot, too," said
Todd. "Come sit on top,"
said Don.

"Look!" said Tom
and Dot.

"It's not hot here!"

12

# Shortstop and the Bug

**by Davis Blackwell**          **Illustrations by Tuko Fujisaki**

What is it, Shortstop?

It's just a small bug.

Can Shortstop grab it? Smash.

Crash! Where's the bug?

The bug is in the dish. Smash.

Crash! You missed it, Shortstop.

The bug hops to the fish.

Oh, no!

**Shortstop, not the fish!**

Splash! The fish is OK,

but where is the bug?

The bug hops off.

Too bad, Shortstop.

# A Big Hit

by Nancy Chiong

Illustrations by
Nathan Jarvis

"Come help me, Bob.

This is a big task."

Gramps and Bob go to the attic. They find good things.

Bob finds a bag. A bat
and a ball are in the bag.

# He and Gramps go play ball.

Bob hits the ball. CRACK!

"It was a grand slam, Bob.
Now let's go back to the
attic and pick up!"

# Pig's Good Morning

by
Davis Blackwell

Illustrations by
Jason Wolff

"This is a good morning,"
snorted Pig.

"Not this morning," said
Cat. "There is a storm."

"Let's play in the corn,"
said Pig.

"No, not now," said Dog.

"There is a storm."

Drip-drop-drip. "The storm
is here!" said Pig.

"Come on, Pig!

We can play in here."

"This is a good morning
for a storm," snorted Pig.

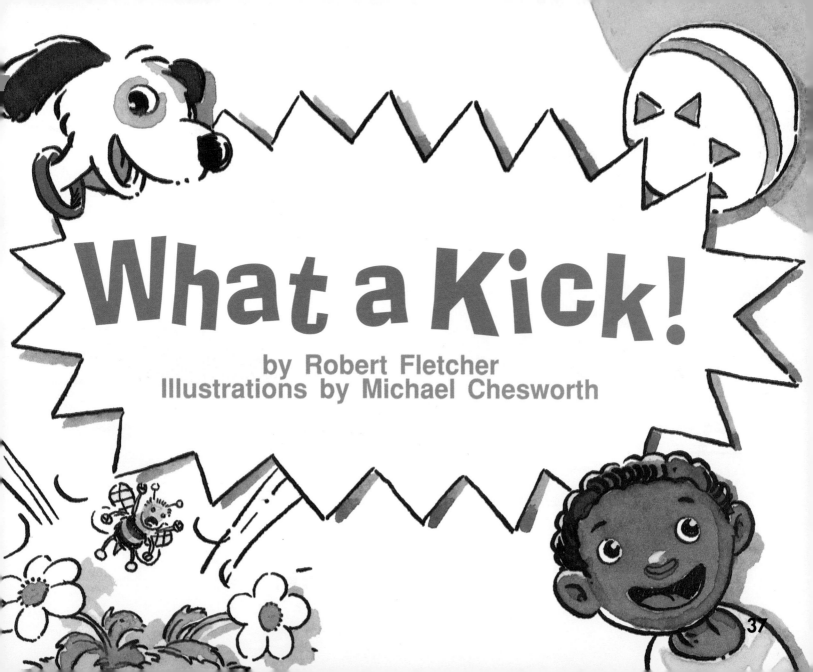

# What a Kick!

by Robert Fletcher
Illustrations by Michael Chesworth

**Mick can kick.**

I can not kick.

Good kick, Mick!

I can not kick.

That is a big kick.

Now Mick is sad.

Here it is, Mick!